MW01517845

Life...
You Can Do It:
Coloring Your World through Adversity

Sheridon "Donna" Palmer

WESTBOW
PRESS®
A DIVISION OF THOMAS NELSON
& ZONDERVAN

WestBow Press books may be ordered through booksellers or by contacting:

WestBow Press
A Division of Thomas Nelson & Zondervan
1663 Liberty Drive
Bloomington, IN 47403
www.westbowpress.com
1 (866) 928-1240

Scripture quotations marked (KJV) taken from the King James Version of the Bible.

ISBN: 978-1-9736-6987-6 (sc)
ISBN: 978-1-9736-6988-3 (hc)
ISBN: 978-1-9736-6986-9 (e)

Library of Congress Control Number: 2019910728

Print information available on the last page.

WestBow Press rev. date: 07/31/2019

Dedicated to my mother, Bethune S. Palmer, who has taught me how to love and appreciate the beauty of life.

Contents

Acknowledgments

Special thanks to my dear mother, Bethune S. Palmer, from Darliston, Jamaica, the family matriarch. A strong, dedicated, and determined woman of God, she continues to fight life mentally, spiritually, and physically. This book is dedicated to her simply for her teachings and guidance from birth and beyond.

Thanks to my dear father, John Alfred Palmer, a fighter and survivor of life. I also want to thank my siblings: Faith Marie Collins; Leovertour "Johnny" Palmer; Leighton "Ali" Palmer; and the twins, Patricia Palmer and Pamela Campbell. They have been my tower of strength and biggest cheerleaders as I journey through the pilgrim pathway of life. Thanks for supporting and allowing me to express my love for life by putting smiles on faces, because you all have come to know that I live to replicate the words of the late Maya Angelou: "My mission in life is not merely to survive, but to thrive; and to do so with some passion, some compassion, some humor, and some style."

To my editing team, Veronica Maragh-Ward (entrepreneur), Trevor B. Nelson (attorney-at-law), and Winsome Lawson (teacher), hats off to you for your dedication and professionalism in reviewing my work.

Introduction

The cycle of life—yes, everyone has a story, whether bitter, sweet, bad, good, unbelievable, spectacular, or senseless. Life is the greatest schoolmaster; it equips, strengthens, and molds us into pioneers, survivors, and leaders. We are not immune or exempt from the circumstances of life. Regardless of race, beliefs, or socioeconomic background, everyone's life experience teaches lessons designed to build and shape our purpose and destiny. We are in this life together and can all learn from each other. Life is made complex by the interaction we have with family and friends and how we deal with our struggles.

We learn from babies—how they cling to the mother's breast for nurture and comfort, how they cry for attention when they are hurting, uncomfortable, or just bored. We learn from the ants—how they prepare way ahead of time for the days when life's resources get scarce and limited, and how they bond together and enable support to carry great treasures of unbelievable sizes. We learn from the homeless—how they gather scraps and garbage to serve as food, shelter, or clothing; and how their bodies can adjust to their situation and biologically stop major functions from occurring. We learn from prisoners—how through survival of the fittest, they can learn how to endure harsh circumstances while locked away in isolation; and how they are able to maximize the opportunity to improve their educational status during incarceration. We learn from the stranded and kidnapped—how they can strive and survive on pure hope that they will be found and rescued soon. We learn from the hungry victims of natural disasters—how they can survive for days just on the thought that they will eat in the near future.

If you are heading in the wrong direction in your life, it's time to make a drastic U-turn. It is no big deal; don't worry about who might be paying attention to your journey. Remember, you are at the wheel of your life, and only you can redirect your route. Everyone makes poor decisions at some juncture of life, but let me be the first to cheer you on this pivotal decision to take a detour. It is never too late. Trust me; you won't regret this decision. It's no mistake that you are reading this book today. To the teenager struggling with peer pressure, bullying, or identity crisis, know that these distractions, although they seem real, are actually illusions. You are in full control of your destiny. Bullies are weak and insecure individuals, who often tend to agitate the person who highlights their shortcomings. Most times, they are just jealous of your strength, intellect, and talents. Your unique identity is your anchor. Never believe the faded voices of the enemy. Share your struggles with a trusted friend or relative. Never feel like no one will understand. Adults were once teenagers. Rest assured that you are not alone. We are all in this together. Chapter 1, The Mirror, focuses on self-esteem and will serve as a guide to help you find and appreciate who you are.

Many adults have and will encounter difficult challenges and unfair breaks in life; yes, those situations can diminish your self-worth. If you are depressed or suffering from fear and anxiety, please stop and reflect on the positives. It doesn't matter whether you are an addict, a rejected spouse, or even an accomplice of a horrible crime; once there is life, there is hope. If you committed a crime, it is only right for you to pay your dues to society for your wrongdoing. However, everyone facing trying times should try to focus on affirmations that can help with his or her mind-set and actions. Suicide isn't an option but simply a false solution. Only when you do not know your purpose does death seems like an option. Ending your life will only make everything worse for the loved ones left behind.

Come on now; let this moment be your day. The only one taking notes of your life is *you*. Don't believe the lies echoing in your head or the lies you have been told. Take a deep breath and immediately start to color your world with hope, peace, and love. No drug, person, job, sickness, or situation is worth your precious life. You are a winner already. Can't you hear the violins and cymbals chiming? Your angels are already celebrating your smart decision to change for the better. So get up and face the sun, face the day, face the world. Start counting your blessings, write them down, and smile at the memories. Take life one hour at a time; yes, you will make the day, you will make the week, you will make the month, and you will make many wonderful years to come.

It is obvious that natural disasters can cause much disruption, loss, and stress to mankind, but they can also bring unity, love, and strength in times of distress. I can recall a few decades ago when a major hurricane swept through South Florida and caused havoc in my hometown. After the devastation, everyone was without power for weeks, but fortunately my apartment was one of the few places that had a gas stove. So guess what? My humble home became the hub for cooking and preparing hot meals for many. Sharing and caring were manifested as we worked together to make a painful situation bearable for each other. I found it enlightening that this unfortunate situation of life was able to unify the community and bring hope and joy.

The battlefield of life can be rather challenging, and I understand that the pressures of life can be overwhelming. However, it seems only wise to use those essentials that are common to us to help soothe the wounds of life.

Energy is the strength and vitality required for sustained or mental activity. In this life we are surrounded with a lot of negative and disturbing energy, but if you are reading this book, it's time to declutter and start painting your life with positive energy. Start removing the thoughts, things, and people in your world that sap your zest, enthusiasm, and vitality. Look at the birds, at how they sway and frolic in the air, extending their wings to the core of the air. Notice the stars—how they shine brightly and radiantly, even when the sky is gloomy and gray. Admire the flowers—how they rhythmically move backward and forward, and bloom despite the humid conditions of the day. To expand our world, we must be intentional about what and who we allow to invade our minds, thoughts, and space. No cynical manipulation should be allowed to distract our mental state. We have to release the energy that complements our inner being.

Nature is inspiring. It is a language that caresses our inner souls. It brings peace and tranquility to mankind, especially in times of distress. If you take a moment to admire nature, you will see the beauty and awesomeness of creation. The sun, moon, stars, clouds, seas, rivers, and plants remind us daily that as humans every source exists to help us survive and strive in life. My mom is a nature lover and is always exclaiming that nature is a true reflection of God, so our family finds nature therapeutic. She has a green thumb, so whatever she plants strives and flourishes, although Mom believes wholeheartedly that her plants and vegetables strive simply because she talks to them and shows them love. Her beautiful, lush garden embodies her passion. Whatever the reason, it is obvious that life is displayed in a magnificent form that creates a calming environment. My family embraces nature by enjoying the beauty and natural form of water. It is customary that every family gathering must involve a trip to the beach, river, mineral bath, falls, or wherever there is water. The beauty of nature complements the luster of life. It rejuvenates the mind, body, and soul; and most importantly, it lends peace.

With technology and imagination, there are many pastimes, such as mindfulness meditation, water therapy, art illusions, board trivia, video games, and word puzzles that can enhance our private worlds. Take, for instance, the genres of music such as jazz, gospel, orchestra, reggae, musical theater, instrumental psychedelic, and rock, to name a few. Some say music is life. It gives peace, inspiration, and hope. It speaks to the inner man. It brings back memories. It reclaims hope. Music can comfort the mind of the suicidal, the discouraged, the hopeless, the rejected, the jealous, the competitive, the angry, the sick, or the depressed person. My nephew has a natural talent for creating musical sounds and arrangements. He is obsessed with the sound of melody. He admires the power of the rhythm, and he invests time and energy by basking in the beauty of musical harmony. Obviously, he is coloring his world by embracing the art of the music genre and creating life-changing songs to match his emotions and experiences. Find the genre that satisfies your mind and promise yourself to live your life to the fullest.

This inspirational book, *Life … You Can Do It*, is just another reminder that "forming the knit," "walking the journey," and "claiming your destiny" are all attainable goals to color your world through adversity. I encourage every reader to focus from this point on the premise that although life comes with many challenges, it is also interesting, intriguing, and wonderful. Once you are breathing, there is always a glimmer of hope and relief. With this mind-set, you will wake up every day, cherishing the fact that life is a special gift to be lived, treasured, and preserved.

Part 1

Forming the Knit

Chapter 1

The Mirror (Self-Effect)

Life does not require that we be the best,
only that we try our best.

—H. Jackson Brown Jr.

*A*cceptance of oneself is a powerful weapon for tackling life. This first chapter was meticulously crafted to allow you to focus on yourself and highlight the positive qualities you possess. Reality check starts in the mirror. What you see is what you get—happy, sad, fat, slim, evil, or kind—but what you do with the reflection in the mirror is paramount: accept, improve, and impart. We have to learn to love ourselves before we can love anyone or anything else. The self-effect is a powerful method to practice to know yourself beyond what others see or tell you.

Children on the path to a great future start by loving the little images in the mirror; they sing and dance in the mirror and admire themselves. It is okay. Let them be. The eyes are the windows of our souls. The mirror has been my best friend and confidante ever since I was conscious of me. I talk to it. I cry in it. I smile with it. I improve me in it. Oh yes, this is the place of truth. It is important to be aware of yourself, including your strengths, weaknesses, preferences, and flaws. Look in the mirror and start loving the image portrayed. Look carefully, and you will be amazed by what you might see, such as strength, courage, determination, and drive.

We all deserve peace and tranquility, which contribute to our self-worth and confidence. This Dalai Lama quote says it best: "Never let the behavior of others destroy your peace." Peace is freedom from disturbances, and we all deserve this perfect state of mind. One technique to pursue inner peace is to release your mind of situations that stifle and disturb your sanity and health. I luxuriate in my peace and enjoy a good night's rest. I will not toss and turn all night, bottled up with disgust and misery for years, only to protect an abuser or an unhealthy situation. Some critics might label me as direct and impetuous, because it's common knowledge to those who know me that if something bothers me to the point of restlessness, I will speak out and address the situation promptly. I cannot entertain the burden of suffering in silence because of someone's abuse, ignorance, or insecurities. I refuse to walk around bombarded with issues that distort my thinking, personality, or vision for my life.

Self-development helps to boost your confidence and allows you to face the truth about yourself. The mirror is a true reflection. It has no filter, and it is true to you and only you. I find that people spend a huge amount of time and energy focusing on the faults of others and at times walk around believing the deception that they are perfect individuals. But the truth is that we all have flaws and should turn our attention to developing our strengths so we can become better people, friends, relatives, and citizens of the universe.

In my family, we are encouraged to take pride in ourselves, not in a form of self-indulgence but as a means to teach us how to appreciate and care for ourselves as special treasures from God. Let me mention at this juncture the importance of maintaining a healthy self-esteem, which is loving yourself without excuse. Self-love is accepting, forgiving, and being kind to you. One can always measure the health of people's self-esteem by their reactions to a camera held in front of them. If you think about it, a camera is really a mirror because in a few seconds you will see a replica of yourself. Hiding from the camera or announcing how much you hate pictures speaks volumes about your fear of what the camera will capture. If you don't like the reflection in the mirror, then do something about it. Don't create a fiasco of your image. On the contrary, build your confidence, which in essence will help you believe in your worth, abilities, and dreams.

An unhealthy self-esteem can fester insecurity and self-pity, which will eventually make you bitter, toxic, and envious. To counteract those ugly traits, don't waste your life resenting others who are living fulfilling lives. Instead, focus on yourself in a positive manner. We all have something we would like to change about our physiques, but it is wise to make peace with your perceived ideology and accept yourself for who you are. Having cosmetic adjustments will make you appear beautiful, but it is how you feel from within that empowers and radiates the true you. That is why for years I have been investing in self-help books for additional motivation to sharpen my self-esteem. To build your self-confidence, identify the qualities you are good at and work harder to be great at them. Don't worry about what others have to say. Words are like vapors. They are powerless. Only your reaction can bring life to negative comments. Work on eliminating the negatives in your life and focus on building a positive empire.

To examine your self-esteem, you need discipline, truth, and courage as necessary tools to identify any hidden imperfections you could be facing. However, to start this tedious process, you must acknowledge and address the vices you struggle with daily. A vice is a negative character trait or habit that tends to control one's emotions. A vice can also be categorized as any addiction ranging from sugar to alcohol, pornography, swearing, anger, smoking, promiscuity, gossip, and even social media. It's any behavior that negates your persona and subtracts from you as a person. Many vices remain clandestine, and most people wouldn't openly admit to the struggle. An alcoholic may be the first to say he or she isn't addicted to liquor; the same is true for the gossiper. Denial is the tool humans use to suppress or ignore the elephants in the room. In most cases, we become comfortable with the vice and accept the practice as a norm. At times, loved ones or even friends are embarrassed by the unacceptable behavior of their loved ones and occasionally in good faith call out the people to try to help them. Let us not wait until someone points out our shortcomings, which could land us in an awkward position. Let us make a deliberate effort to address these vices and improve as people.

To eradicate these negative behavioral traits, it's imperative to start dissecting them. To dissect anything is painful and messy, but eventually the pain will subside and bring relief and joy. Recently, I had a splinter in my foot. It was annoying and painful, but I had to examine the source of pain and address the situation immediately, which meant aggressively removing the foreign object. Once the object was released, I had my liberty to walk around pain free with poise and grace. Anything dissected will result in a better outcome. Don't allow anything or anyone to hold your freedom captive.

Low self-esteem is a monster that robs someone of the essence of life. I have a friend who suffered from low self-esteem for most of her life and admitted that for years she dodged having her photo taken, because she despised the images they captured. After her divorce, she started working on her self-worth and eventually became a picture fanatic. Without having knowledge of her lifelong struggle, some might have misunderstood her newfound hobby and might even have judged her wrongfully. But she remained oblivious to the naysayers because she recognized her weakness. She realized that the practice of taking pictures and admiring herself was ultimately unraveling years of insecurity while helping to carve a healthier self-image. You need to be radical about who you want to become and work earnestly at it, despite the harsh criticisms or comments of the onlookers. Those onlookers are there only to test your impetus and willpower. I say do you boo. The camera is magical, so relax, smile, and let it capture the image. It might just surprise you.

The mirror is your best friend because it doesn't judge you. On the contrary, it keeps your secrets, crazy looks, weird hairdos, covered-up bulges, and scared countenance. The mirror is my place of incision, where I chip away at my fears, thoughts, and flaws. In so doing, I have learned about the attributes that have molded me as a person. You are your biggest cheerleader. No one knows you like you do. You know your strengths, weaknesses, mistakes, secrets, talents, shortcomings, and yourself. Be yourself.

For me, my challenge was hearing my recorded voice. I was never comfortable listening to myself on a voice message. However, my frightening eye-opener was a few years ago when I was privileged to toast a bride at a wedding. After the event, everyone complimented me on the beautiful delivery and presentation. However, my reality check came a few weeks later when I had a chance to privately watch the video and carefully listen to my speech. Honestly, this was painful to watch, but guess what? I didn't wallow for long, critiquing myself. Instead, I initiated an action plan to build on that negative streak. I started practicing every day. Even though no one was aware that I struggled with this flaw, I was determined to conquer it. From listening to myself repeatedly, I discovered that I had to speak more slowly and carefully listen to myself until I felt confident and satisfied with the sound of my voice.

By indulging in knowing me, I have discovered that I am a people person and take pleasure in investing in the well-being of others. This quality of caring has become an asset to my persona, and subsequently, I try to maintain that standard and make every effort to be a positive influence on whomever I encounter on my journey. Of course, a little favoritism is sprinkled when it comes to my nieces and nephews. For them I aim to be honest and sincere with my compliments, advice, and concerns. Giving praises and adoration continues to be my focus while instilling in them the power of a healthy self-esteem. I reinforce how, as they grow older, believing in themselves can channel them to attain great heights. I can recall some years ago when my youngest niece, only eight years old at the time, called to let me know she had a school assignment to write about someone she admired. She wanted to write about me. Of course, the thought was flattering, but I was also honored and happy to know she'd chosen me. It was apparent that without my knowledge, I was making a positive impact on her.

If you are the type of person who internalizes everything and suffers alone in a relationship, a career, or even your own limitations, today is the opportune time to recognize any shortcomings you might have accepted as normal behavior. Make a vow to change. Never succumb to the belief that because of your personality type, you cannot be bold or defend yourself. Find the courage to face the inner demons in your private or public lives and aim to strengthen yourself. Be aware that once you rid your life of fear, insecurity, and doubt, everyone will admire your enhancement and eventually develop more respect for your perseverance to improve. Whatever life throws your way, be determined to fight for yourself because you know you deserve better and more.

> I will go anywhere as long as it's forward.
> —David Livingston

Chapter 2

Family Fusion

Family is not an important thing. It's everything.

—Michael J. Fox

I totally believe that a loving, caring family is the core of a successful life. Family should not only refer to your biological association but anyone who has embraced, supported, encouraged, or loved you unconditionally. The love and energy of family are powerful attributes to motivate anyone to keep on going. I was raised in an exceptional family with Christian parents and five siblings. We were taught that a praying family can overcome any obstacle, and yes, we have proved that time and time again. My mother instilled in us that if one cries, we all cry; and if one hurts, we all hurt. That mantra has framed our family fusion.

Everyone and everything attached to our family fusion are embraced, cherished, and respected. Our pets have special names and are crafted in the circle as special. Rover, Blackie, Bruno, Rexi, Husky, Lassie, Chloe, and Fluff are just some of the endearing names of our dogs. These pets taught us the value of life by how they cared and nurtured their pups and environment. Isn't it strange how even animals are protective of life? Yet there are mentally stable humans who casually waste and abuse the precious gift of life, oblivious to the fact that time wasted is time lost.

We had no choice into which family we are born, and like anything else in life, it takes work to create a beautiful fusion. All families encounter life challenges; we just never know the magnitude of what our neighbor is dealing with. For some families it might be known issues such as a tragedy, incarceration, terminal illness, or effects of a natural disaster, but for many their challenges remain unknown to the world. Life isn't partial, and no one is exempt from the woes of life. Every family at some stage of life faces different levels of distress, embarrassment, pain, or crisis.

It's fair to say that most of us are unaware what other families go through on a daily basis. Never be fooled by the smiles and facade people plaster about their families. Every day families of all dimensions are dealing with some type of secret issues ranging from ill-health, rebellious relatives, financial strains, criminal offences, or even incestuous encounters.

I believe the secret to getting through the rough patches as a family is simply to huddle together and practice love and kindness. You would be surprised how just a simple smile or compliment can soften the blows of life's challenges. In our family, laughter is fostered to lighten our troubles. We focus on making every family member feel loved, happy, accepted, and supported. My parents always reminded us that the family that sticks together can conquer every roadblock life brings.

Bonding is practiced in our family by allowing us to be ourselves, to open up and share our passion of what drives us. We promote the slogan "Dare to be different, dare to be you." We believe the complexity of family is the joy of family. My family comes with a myriad of personalities. Game nights always reveal the depth of our personalities, especially during Scrabble, one of our favorite word games. These occasions bring out the competitive streaks. We have the calculated executive siblings; the jovial, competitive in-laws; the loving, adventurous nephews; and then the outgoing, confident nieces. But all personalities contribute to the happiness and joy that frame our core. As for my siblings, all five carry special qualities necessary to keep each other grounded and confident. My oldest sister, who prides herself in being the "chief advisor" for the family, a title she earned from my father, is a natural leader whom everyone confides in for counsel and direction. The family respects her role and acts accordingly because we totally appreciate her tact and wisdom. Another stalwart in the family is my youngest brother, who loves the world and shows his charm to everyone from the priest to the pauper. My mother refers to him as the "street boy," not to be seen in an abject manner but rather as a quasi mayor for the community, who has a unique mission to unite and care for humanity. I, on the other hand, have an animated personality and have been called effervescent, exuberant, and vivacious. I welcome all descriptions with open arms, because these are the qualities that have funneled my positive involvement in the lives of my family. Every family member has his or her own individual journey and must be comfortable to express who he or she is and never feel judged or ridiculed.

Many times we as adults fail at nurturing our young because we are so consumed with the pressures of life, but the sad reality is that by being sidetracked, we lose family members, especially the youths. In this cyberage, when the challenges of date rape, addiction, identity crisis, and mental health are prevalent, some adults out of ignorance can appear callous to the genuine concerns our youths face on a regular basis. We must take time to educate ourselves regarding this dilemma. By dedicating time to listen to them, we inevitably create lasting bonds. Investing in the younger generation is of prime importance, because truth be told, they are the future and will be making important decisions about our universe after we are gone. These special occasions serve as inspiration for me, and I try to maintain a healthy rapport with my nieces and nephews, because I have come to realize that a positive connection is important to building trust and confidence with the younger generation.

When my younger nephew was born, I developed a special bond with him. I can remember taking long trips during the cold December months just to celebrate his birthday. To see the smile on his tiny face sufficed for the sacrifices made to be there in person. Because of this connection, he always felt safe and secure, sharing whatever fears and troubles he faced during his school years. Even today, the relationships I have maintained with my now-adult nephews have helped to assure them that they can always rely on me, regardless of whatever phase of life they are experiencing.

In our family circle, celebration of life is encouraged. We celebrate health, wealth, accomplishments, and even challenges, because we realize that even the valley experiences are necessary to shape our lives. Birthdays are evidence of another shot at life, and they are cherished in our family circle. Growing up, we were exempt from our routine chores on our birthdays, and our family used this prime opportunity to remind the birthday celebrant that he or she was special, unique, admired, and important in this life. This practice has been deliberately embedded in my DNA, and to date I have never worked on my birthday (no way). I treat my birthday as a day to reflect, retreat, and reshape my life.

Another important factor of family life is accepting the "adopted" family members. Personally, I don't have any biological children, but I have mentored and nurtured many boys and girls alike. However, there was a special young lady who became part of our lives for over twenty-five years. She was like the daughter I never had. She gravitated to me and even called me the endearing term *mom*. We shared many hurts, pains, joys, and secrets; and even as a grown woman, I refer to her children as my grandchildren. Although we're not related biologically, nothing between us can separate the love and bond we share. How ironic that later in life, we realized her biological mother was a Palmer before she got married. *Talk about the surprises of life.* Well, maybe our similarities in taste, traits, behavior, and likeness weren't coincidental, but the possibility that our family genes have been mixed in the wonders of heredity puzzles. However, even without that discovery, our family bond remains stronger and authentic.

Take a look at your family circle and dissect the positive qualities of each member. Appreciate the differences among yourselves and remember that in life, no two persons are alike. We are all unique in our own ways. Family is special and heartwarming, but as mentioned in the popular Bible story of jealousy and envy among Joseph and his brothers, I have seen, read, and heard of family members hating, backbiting, robbing, and even killing each other over earthly possessions and trivial matters. Remember that material things are only temporary gifts that will decay and rot, so if you find yourself in the midst of such family feuds, forgive them all, move on, and live anyway.

Chapter 3

Power of Friendship

Love all, trust a few, do wrong to none.
—William Shakespeare

*F*riends, we've got to love them. I have a large fan base of friends, some more special than others. Some brought their problems, while others brought their passions. Friends exist to help us grow, glow, and enjoy life, but they can also burden, drain, and suffocate us. We all need a variety of friends, but it really comes down to the super core … those loyal, trustworthy, and supportive angels who connect with our vision, support our mission, and encourage our goals. For years I held the title of "CEO of the World," trying to fix everyone's problems and concerns, until I met a dear friend from Europe who seriously opened my eyes as to where I was falling short on my purpose. He ministered to me wholeheartedly for months to help me define and refine my life. He prayed with me, cried with me, traveled with me, played with me, shared with me, and struggled with me. Sometimes it's the person whom you least expect to have an indelible impact on your life who actually hits the spot. What a revelation: a friend in need is a friend indeed.

Friendships are divine flowers in our lives, yet deception, jealousy, strife, and envy are just a few of the ugly vipers that creep their way in to abolish the friendship bond, but live anyway. Betrayal is inevitable; we will encounter it, but use it as a learning tool and live anyway. In life we make unbearable sacrifices to build relationships and give until there is nothing left, yet the partner whom you thought was an angel turns out to be your worst nightmare, but live anyway. The friend, who seemed to care and sympathize with all your disappointments and mistakes, turned out to be your biggest traitor, but live anyway. And let me not forget our coworkers; that peer who taught you all the tricks and trades on your career path turned out to be the deceiver who took your position, but lived anyway. Ladies, not all women are jealous, conniving, or mean; and gentlemen, not all male friends are insecure, competitive, or rude. We have to try the friendships and discern those who are right for us, depending on what stage we are in life. Some friends are meant to stay, while others are definitely only for a season.

Never underestimate the power of a stranger. God allows people to come into our lives for different reasons. Some are long term; others are maybe only for a moment. Let us stop and reflect on the quality of friends we have and how they are impacting our purpose. I embrace positivity and continue to encourage meaningful, positive thinking among my family members and colleagues. Through situations we can embrace life's mishaps and build forever relationships.

I am reminded of a much older lady, who was diagnosed with a terminal disease during the latter stage of her life. We were acquainted from social circles but had never had a friendship per se. She was a fierce, strong-willed, and—might I add—unforgiving woman, whom many shunned to avoid conflicts. I was touched by her courage to fight this disease and later became her closest counterpart; that's when I learned about her struggles and disappointments, and then realized why she had such anger, bitterness, and hatred toward mankind. But after going through the vigorous treatment plan and experiencing the love of strangers (myself being one), the love of God and the love of life, she was convinced, revived, and changed to fulfill her purpose. Life has a way of teaching us harsh lessons to connect us to our destiny, and that is what makes it so intriguing.

Another close friend of mine, same age-group and a solid woman of God, experienced a nasty relationship mishap from a Christian minister. Expectations are necessary life tools, but they can also be dream killers if you're not grounded, focused, and strong in the Lord. Life served her some nasty medicines, some undeserving and cold, but she kept her faith in God through tears, depression, and fasting; and she pushed past her circumstances. I was there for her through thick and thin, sometimes burdened and scared, but she needed a true friend to help her through the rough times. She talked for hours every single day. Did I say hours? Oh yes, sometimes six to seven hours, not only talking about her divorce situation but also about life in general—the good, the bad, and the ugly. We had thought-provoking conversations. We learned from each other. We prayed together, and of course we fought together, all in good faith.

Then there are the angels who come along the pathway of life to brighten my path as I journey through life. I personally have a barrage of girlfriends, whom I cherish dearly. Those from high school, who appear after decades, and it seems like we never skipped a day. Some were roommates who helped with my schoolwork, designed my outfits, created my hairdos, or even clandestine schemes and strategies; whatever the purpose, my girlfriends are super special. I remember one of my milestone birthdays when I gathered relatives and a group of close girlfriends for a weekend getaway … just to celebrate life with me. In anticipation of the big weekend, we had months of competition for losing weight, prepping outfits, and gathering jokes. On the first day of the celebration, my big sister had the brilliant idea to feed my passion for surprises. She had it arranged for my baby sister, my confidante and guiding angel, to drive miles from home to surprise me at the resort. This reveal was an awesome feeling, mixed with wonderful emotions just to have her share in this memorable event.

While at the resort, we told stories, shared our wishes, and laughed at each other's jokes, flaws, and quirks. We cried with those who were hurting, basked in the crystal waters of the ocean, and of course danced and ate everything provided at the resort. Oh, what a wonderful time of togetherness. No one was there to judge or criticize, just to create times of tasteful, blissful memories. One of the activities I had for the ladies was my "self-improvement purse." Yes, I believe in using every opportunity to reflect, deflect, improve, and grow as a person. So I entrusted my girlfriends to be honest with me and write anything about me I should correct, embrace, or delete. I was happy and impressed by some of the kind, powerful comments written on those little bits of paper about my influence and inspiration. I got many words of encouragement, and of course, I had the brutally honest comments that have totally helped me to become a better person. Ladies, you all know who you are. Thank you for that memorable weekend, which remains indelible in my heart. Honestly, I still reminisce on the fifty-plus hours we spent together.

As a single woman, male friends are honorary too. They keep me balanced, confident, and whole. Some remain to be admirers, but they are mature, respectable, and kind gentlemen who are smart enough to understand the delicacy and importance of not ruining genuine friendships. My male counterparts are there to give me their honest opinions and perspectives, which I appreciate and hold dear when making life decisions.

One important life lesson I have learned is that success will surely shine the light on the real cheerleaders in your life. The more you succeed, the more friends will sever from your surroundings. Don't be dismayed; you are on the right track. You aren't doing anything wrong; you are actually doing something right. I learned that most friends will remain excited for you when your life is mediocre, but the moment you start to soar to higher dimensions, the separation begins. Be aware that this concept holds true in every area of life. A quote from Justbestcovers.com says it just right: "Success can breed fake friends and true enemies, so keep your circle tight." Your circle, with family and friends alike, should always want to see you win and clap loudly when you succeed. If that isn't the case, especially for your friends, then I'm afraid it's time to form a new circle.

Part 2

Walking the
Journey

Chapter 4

The Fight (Life Effect)

Challenges, failures, defeats and ultimately,
progress, are what make your life worthwhile.
—Maxime Lagacé

*A*popular gospel song says, "No one said it would be easy." You're right: life is a constant fight and struggle—only hard work and perseverance will prevail. Great men like Warren Buffett and Nelson Mandela taught me that what you put in is what you will surely get out. I grew up reciting this sought-after quote by poet Henry Wadsworth Longfellow: "The heights by great men reached and kept were not attained by sudden flight, but they, while their companion slept, were toiling upward in the night." To toil is to work hard with a strategic plan to fulfill a purpose. It is imperative to tackle life with an attitude of steadfastness. Don't follow those in their slumber but dare to intercept the fight with resilience. It is excruciating and humiliating to lose anything in life, but come on now; put on your imaginary boxing gloves and fight. Fight for your mind, health, sanity, family, marriage, and career. Fight for your life. It is worth it.

Competition is one of those sneaky demons that robs the beauty and essence of your life, because during your time of competing with the Joneses, you are ultimately losing focus of your purpose to create change in this world. Don't waste valuable time to peek over the fence. Know that wherever you are at this time is exactly where God ordained you to be. Don't complicate your life with social media, hearsays, or even what people say about you. The pressure of social media is destroying many and giving hope of being popular, authentic, and loved. I have observed over the years that with technology people tend to say and do what they believe others would like to hear or see. Many times what is displayed isn't necessarily as truthful as it appears to be. Deception is prevalent, and we must identify the factors that aim to deceive and distract us from maximizing our full potential. Dig deep for that fight that makes you want to wake up at night to sketch a game plan; this is the fight that makes you reject that delicious piece of chocolate cake, that forces you to avoid senseless gossip, or that lets you seek God beyond your feelings.

Empirical evidence has proved that the fear of failure causes many to forfeit launching out into new horizons. Sometimes our ego, pride, or status hinders us from reaching greater heights. Life has a way of teaching lessons of failure, not because we are incapable, weak, or incompetent; but sometimes if we fail at something, we are forced to try harder or try something different. Yes, failure is painful and real, but failure also exists to build our character, stamina, and mental state. More often than not, failure has propelled people into their destiny and fate. A lot of these people end up writing their stories to encourage and motivate others. Whatever the circumstance, don't allow fear to cripple your goals and aspirations. Great men and women, before and after our time, have failed over and over again, but after many errors they have succeeded in perfecting the task. There are many options in life; write down the truth behind your fears, talk them over with a true friend or family member, pray for strength and direction, and be inspired to go for *your* goal. You won't regret it. If your plan A fails, then start a plan B, then C, and go all the way to Z. Start over if you must but never roll over and accept failure as your final answer.

We need our jobs and strive to succeed in our careers. Being an executive of the corporate world, I can attest to the fact that there are many challenges with coworkers, business partners, and even employers. How ironic that many of us have been hurt miserably the moment our career started to escalate. In light of promotion, favor, and success, there is also deception, racism, discrimination, disrespect, lies, and plots. These realities are all common in the workplace to block and discourage progress. Know that leadership is an art that brings out our unique, diamond qualities, so don't be sidetracked by challenges on the job. Remind yourself daily that those obstacles are there only to sway you away from your destiny. I am well aware that these elements exist and are valid roadblocks that deter progress in our work lives. I truly want to admonish you to abolish those thoughts that have you thinking these unfortunate occurrences are based solely on your race, sex, ethnic background, sexual preference, religious belief, political affiliation, or physical appearance. Most times these deterrents are multifaceted and may not be correlated to your status. Whenever the opportune time arises for that promotion, relationship, business deal, or breakthrough, there is nothing under the sun that can avoid it from existing. Learn to trust time. A friend of mine published an interesting book titled *The Advantage of Now*. In his book he carefully expounded on the process and benefits of timing. Don't focus on the adversaries. Remember, people can be selfish and ungrateful. Hurting people hurt others; users are abusive and narcissists are manipulative.

Resiliency is strength. Many business leaders today have shared compelling stories of greed, deceit, and prejudice, which they have experienced throughout their careers. However, these incidents are only temporary blockers, which if conquered will ultimately make us stronger and more prepared for the next career move.

It's apparent that these leaders would all concur that they had to fight day and night to accomplish their desired goals. Remember that the mind is the most powerful organ we own, and we have the power to direct our focus on the positive possibilities ahead. Only you can determine how you allow these betrayals, hurts, or disappointments to affect your life pattern. Don't spend your precious days pondering the job you lost or the deal that fell through. At times, winning the fight, getting that deal, or scoring a ten necessitates additional knowledge and training. A powerful remedy to counteract the fight is to nourish your mind and brain cells; invest in education, learn a new skill, or find an area of interest and become an expert on the subject matter. Do the research and find applicable opportunities to enhance yourself. There are universities, trade schools, or even self-development centers that offer affordable and, in some cases, free courses to help equip those interested in succeeding. Knowledge coupled with perseverance is a sure recipe for winning.

Life is known to throw bitter stones our way; oh yes, and these can bring depression, frustration, and even suicidal thoughts for some. Suicide is never an option; it is just a thought wrapped in fear and lies. To the troubled teenager, that bully at school is just a weak, insecure person who is jealous of your strength, brilliance, and beauty. Bullies strive only when you entertain their lame tactics. Your life is worth so much more, and no one should have power over you. Just think about the loved ones—your little brother, little sister, cousins, parents, and grandparents—who love, admire, and look to you for inspiration and motivation. Snap that damaging thought and replace it immediately with hope and possibilities. Avoid making a permanent decision because of a temporary situation. Be reminded that there are many options available to help you overcome that dark, dull period in your life. Challenges are designed to make us stronger, smarter, and more resilient. Timing is everything, and at times these rejections are really openings for a greater opportunity. Work hard, strive for success, and ensure that you are consistent in pursuit of your goals, which will ultimately add value and relevance to your life.

I have always told my family and colleagues that I will never deliberately take my life. When you know the value of life and the promises and possibilities lying ahead, you treasure and guard your life beyond all odds. Be gentle with yourself; pamper your mind, body, and soul. Indulge in "me" times; create a spa day at home, love on your family, friends, neighbors, and even some strangers. We all inhabit this beautiful planet, so let us be deliberate and explore it. Slow down and rejuvenate your inner being. If you're walking, take a moment and smell the colorful bougainvillea shrubs, play with the friendly squirrels, and admire the beautiful foliage, the peaceful lakes, the majestic skies, or other natural habitats. If you are driving, roll the windows down and enjoy the chiming wind, smell the crisp air, and sing aloud to let your mind exhale. Life is already a challenge. Let us purpose in our minds to enjoy the experiences as they come. Believe me, we are surrounded by enough positives to brighten our world. Most important, foster harmony among all men, pursue peace, and love your neighbors as yourself. Wherever you are planted, promise yourself to bloom and leave a legacy for the next generation.

Chapter 5

Unforgivable Chances or Not?

Love is of all passions the strongest, for it attacks
simultaneously the head, the heart and the senses.

—Lao Tzu

*L*ove is God, and love is beautiful. Love drives our emotions, and as humans we tend to appreciate love and attention in any form it is given, whether from another person or from a pet. However, if we lose the love we once adored, we are inclined to blame ourselves and conduct a daily postmortem to decipher the reason for the loss. Trust and respect are most important in a love affair, and no one deliberately destroys a relationship. Subtle mistakes are made without realizing that as minuscule as these incidents are, they can be detrimental to something special. Finding the perfect mate is every girl's dream to see her Boaz on a white horse and sweeping her off her feet. It's beautiful indeed, but Boaz will appear only when we are ready mentally, emotionally, physically, and spiritually. God checks our motives to prepare us for these special occasions, so let us be reasonable and search our hearts to see whether we are really prepared to accommodate our Boaz.

One could equate unforgivable chances to the one who got away, the one we thought made our world seem complete, fulfilled, and right. Misunderstanding, finances, upbringing or intellect are just a few of the reasons why we suffer in relationships. Sometimes our poor choices are linked to past experiences, which stain and distort our judgment, and cause us to revert to emotional, physical, and even social abuse. No need to entertain senseless dialogue with your ex, trying to amend the inevitable past. Truth be told, if there was enough substance to sustain the relationship, it would be striving today. Remember, nothing lost was ever meant for you.

The gloomy reality of relationships is that there are also rejection, hurt, and disappointments. At some stage in relationships, we retrospect, blame, grow apart, and eventually leave. Reality stares us in the face, and we now realize that the once-burning glee crashes to a painful halt and grinds to a crushing end. Relational suicides and rejection can cause sleepless nights, weight loss or weight gain, isolation, confusion, uncontrollable weeping, and for some even suicidal thoughts. Pride is really a cunning emotion that drives all these reactions. It is natural to want to protect ourselves, and rightfully so, but why should we succumb to emotional abuse, selfishness, and hurt just because we lost a love we thought was perfect? Isn't it funny how time and time again we encounter folks who share their deepest disgust and unhappiness in a relationship, yet they continue to cling to an abusive, selfish mate only because they fear the thought of being alone?

The month of February is recognized as the month of love, yet many in relationships dread the dawn of Valentine's Day because of the uncertainty, wondering whether they would be treated special and showered with flowers, candy, stuffed animals, or an awesome night out. How ironic that the day meant to bring cupids and happiness seems to bring fear, anxiety, and disappointments to a lot of people. I believe that in life it is those close acquaintances observing our relationships who place great expectations, which usually fuel the anxiety and fear on February 14 for "some" people in committed relationships. It's on this special love day that many relationships falter, because trust is compromised, while on the other hand other relationships flourish because trust is reinforced. But such is life. If you are a victim of such disappointments, use the experience to pamper yourself and find peace. Disappointments are usually a result of failed expectations.

Personally, I have had quality relationships from varying societal backgrounds, many heartaches, and pain; but in the end, it's the heart that matters. Profession, status, and wealth are wonderful elements to make life great, but a beautiful heart can give the feeling of a thousand butterflies in the bowel of your soul and supersede all the above elements. Physical attraction is definitely important in the process but can have the tendency to lead into an Eros-type relationship. True love won't be swayed only by the illusion of your intriguing silhouette or tantalizing body movements. Remember, for the union to strive in a healthy manner, there has to be a deeper connection of the souls.

From experience I learned that it's important to protect one's heart in the whirlwind of emotions, because sheer feeling is only a fallacy that will rob us of sacred agape love—the kind of unselfish love that transcends beyond the natural state of mind; the kind that cares, shares, and forgives without contempt; the kind of love that captures your heart. This agape love will have you do the unthinkable like relocating to another side of the world, with little or no resources, while living under the open canopy just to be with the one you love. In life, it's the heart that allows us to love beyond measure, so remove the notion that feelings alone can bring true satisfaction.

Humans have the propensity to protect their choices, status, or even their mistakes. They tend to justify and speak life into whatever choice they are committing to, even if the decision is contrary to their preference. Take, for instance, buying a home or choosing a mate. If the house seems too small, we verbalize that we never intended to have a huge property because of high maintenance, cost, or other insignificant reasons. However, the moment we find a bigger property we can afford, our lingo immediately changes. The same is true if we are dating an unattractive person or someone with a differing social background; in defense we proclaim that we always loved this type of person only until we fall for someone better or more in sync with our taste or likeness. Never allow outside forces to dominate your emotions or choices. Find the courage to make calculated decisions that are most suitable for your life.

Love is caring and sharing. Love is adoring and making sacrifices. Love isn't selfish but is kind. If you are single, lonely, or divorced, take the time to dissect your past relationships. Ignore the proclivities or thoughts that seem to disturb you in the midnight hours. Be honest with yourself, use this exercise to rebuild your self-confidence, and you will realize you weren't robbed or cheated, but in essence you were spared for a greater encounter. Take time to heal, take time to forgive yourself, and know that despite past rejections, humiliation, and hurt, true love is from God. Rest assured that it will find your heart, and one day you too will soar into the blissful abyss of happiness, joy, and peace. Keep loving yourself, and that special someone will admire your drive and strength; he or she will develop genuine curiosity to explore your inner being.

In closing, no incident in life is unforgivable, not even the love opportunities we lost. Yes, lost love can hurt but find the courage to forgive and forget. Yes, I said forgive. It is proved that forgiveness is all about our peace and not about the other person; however, to forget, in my opinion, could be like a setup to repeat the same mistake. So don't hold grudges, but use these unfortunate pitfalls as lessons learned for the next encounter. Never hold your future hostage to someone who doesn't see your worth or heart. Know that at times the demise of a relationship is better for your sanity and pride.

I concur that it's human to cry, mope and ponder; but it's time to wash away the ugly stains of teardrops from your face and start living again. Like anything else in life, if one door is closed, another will surely open. It might not happen on our timing, but God knows our hearts, and He knows exactly what is good for us. Find the courage and do yourself a favor to heal emotionally, mentally, and spiritually. As difficult as it seems, I have done it, and I know you can do it too, so let him go, let her go, let it go … Your life is worth it.

Chapter 6

Gifts and Talents

You only live once, but if you do it right, once is enough.

—Mae West

*W*e all have gifts and talents to change the world or simply to change one person at a time. If you reflect on your childhood days, you will associate something you enjoyed doing more than anything else, whether it was helping people, creating things, talking to people, leading others, singing, dancing, exploring, or reading. There was that "little something" that felt natural. Yes, intuitively, we realize our innate passion is now the catalyst of our lives.

Gifts and talents are homogeneous and usually defined as natural skills or abilities, such as hairdressing, artwork, body art, singing, poetry, swimming, ice skating, gymnastics—you name it. Gifts are sometimes associated as God given while talents translate to something innate. Some gifts can seem hidden or dormant, but both gifts and talents must be identified, developed, and nurtured for maximum benefits. The popular TV show *America's Got Talent* is noted for giving the young, old, disabled, or even rejected another chance to add luster and color to their lives by showcasing their gifts and talents. Some acts are so unbelievable that they literally blow your mind or leave you gasping for air. I admire the contestants because it takes courage and many trials and errors to enter into such a competitive arena with the confidence of possibly winning the entire competition. This tenacity and drive encourage viewers to push for what they believe they can attain. The show is entertaining but, more so, quite rewarding to see others coloring their lives for different reasons. Some might enter to build the career of their dreams, others simply for self-actualization or fame. But whatever the reason, I love this show because it promotes positivity.

Take for instance the myriad of talents distributed among my immediate family. As a child, my mother, even though she excelled academically and desired to become a nurse or teacher, always had the inclination to design and make women's clothing. Her mother, my grandmother, was a seamstress, but my mom was never taught the art of sewing. As she grew older, she embraced her natural gift and developed a successful career as a neighborhood seamstress. She designed and made an array of clothing to include school uniforms. She also specialized in accessories such as buttons, belts, and buckles. Mom enjoyed her work wholeheartedly and gave back to her community by way of teaching young ladies the art of sewing. Even today, though in her eighties, Mom continues to sew and design outfits. My father also never got formal training but had a natural gift for shoe designing and made a lucrative career that sustained his family. He owned and operated a shoe factory in his hometown. This inspired many young men in the community to learn his craft.

Here's a funny story. My older sister and I were introduced at an early age to formal music lessons on the piano. We were devoted and ventured out many evenings after school to learn how to read the notes and practice our rhythms and chords; but on the contrary, it was my older brother who never had the opportunity to learn playing the piano, but he grew up and naturally played musical notes by ear, simply listening to the melody. The truth is, when my mother was pregnant with my brother, she frequently played the harmonica, a small rectangular wind instrument, without any formal lessons, so my mother believes my brother's gift was developed in his genes while he was still in her womb.

Today my brother is a professional keyboard player at a well-established church, where he serves as the director of music.

My twin sisters are naturally blessed with creativity when it comes to art and crafts. They have created objects and elements that have amazed even professionals in the field. I'm referring to floral arrangements, gift baskets, canvas art, upholstery, and more.

Another naturalist in the family is my oldest niece, who always had an eye for abstract art and has the ability to sketch amazing scenarios freehandedly. Her work transcends beauty and emotional power of strength. We later learned that this talent was hereditary because her father also had a natural gift of the arts and as a young man made artwork and sculptures in the past.

It's also interesting how the grandchildren are gifted and talented. One of my nieces inherited the technique in dress design from her grandmother and excelled in this area during her high school years. She designed her very first dress at the tender age of fourteen; this stylish dress ultimately won first place in a fashion contest. Yet another niece inherited the gift of creativity and writing skills, which I suppose most of the family got from my mother. This niece won the overall prize for the "Best Short Story" in the Caribbean Examination Council (CXC), and earned herself a fully paid scholarship to an accredited law school. Today she practices as a successful attorney and enjoys writing for a living. See how your gift can make room for you if you allow yourself to expand on your natural traits. And how can I forget another niece, who seems to have bones made of cartilage? She has been a gymnastics expert for all her years in high school and gleefully led her school team and represented the team as the "topper" in the creative aerobatic stunts. Although the family feared for her safety, her natural instinct for gymnastics was graceful and flawless. This practice has taken her to many interesting places to include North America, where the team competed with teams from prestigious countries.

I am sharing these examples to show how gifts and talents are embedded into everyone's DNA, and if we tap into them, they can open unbelievable doors. It is therefore our assignment to figure out our innate treasures and earnestly build to highlight the gifts we possess. Popular Olympic stars, such as Michael Phelps in swimming, Serena Williams in tennis, Bradie Tennell in figure skating, and Usain Bolt in athletics are all examples of ordinary people who have unearthed their talents and embraced the endless possibilities that favored them to fame, wealth, and even early retirement.

Talents can be discovered in diverse ways. Walking the streets of big cities, one can always see a plethora of talents sprawling the street corners, such as the amazing saxophone player, the unassuming lady with the melodious voice, the talented impersonator of politicians and popular characters, or the skillful clown juggling balls. Don't feel shy to shine and showcase your gifts and talents because you just never know whom they could motivate or when someone of influence will be fascinated by your act. Just think about the possibilities. A movie production team might just be in the vicinity to hear your singing, see your acting skills, or hear your poetic expressions. Follow your heart and dreams; someone could be waiting to add color to your life.

No matter your age, I know you can jumpstart your gifts and

talents today. I encourage everyone reading this chapter never to bury his or her talents or discourage his or her children from developing their natural gifts. Instead, give support, guidance, and praise because sometimes all it takes is a hand clap or a compliment to motivate someone to push to display his or her talents. Personally, I realize one cannot be totally freed until he or she is operating in his or her congenital element—the divine destiny.

Part 3

Claiming Your Destiny

Chapter 7

Passion and Purpose (Divine Effect)

Don't gain the world and lose your soul,
wisdom is better than silver or gold.

—Bob Marley

*F*ollow the leader. Only He can orchestrate your life and lead you into purpose. Our passion is the fuel that drives our dreams. Follow your heart. Your faith in God is surmountable to all life's challenges and surprises. Our innate passion catapults the eclipse that leads to our purpose in life. Mike Murdock, an American singer, says whatever bothers you is where your purpose lies. For me, it is the burden of life on mankind, whether it's homelessness, sickness, poverty, loneliness, or discrimination. True happiness cannot be attained until you embrace your God-given purpose, which embodies the reason you were created. As a child, I abhorred the thought of lack, pain, or abuse of humans and animals. Now an adult, my heart draws me to the most vulnerable individuals I meet on my journey. Growing up as a toddler, I remember spending countless days in the local hospital, because I had allergic reactions to several foods. During those days, I welcomed visitation from anyone, even strangers. The fact that I can relate to the emptiness of sickness gives me great joy to visit the sick and shut-ins in their homes, institutions, and especially the pediatric wards in hospitals. I find it rewarding to put smiles on faces by showing love and affection

I genuinely show empathy to the homeless lacking food and shelter, to the child who has no love and care, to the person without justice or a voice, or to the elderly who lack family or help. I am guided by the scripture Isaiah 58:10 (*revised standard version*), which says, "If you pour yourself out for the hungry and satisfy the desire of the afflicted, then shall your light rise in the darkness and your gloom be as the noonday." Hunger can be described as a knife viciously piercing the organs with no mercy. Once I identified my purpose, I began praying to God to put situations in my path so I could make a difference in someone's life. It warms my heart to put smiles on faces; hence, for years I started making sacrifices to promote my mission by being instrumental in giving back to mankind. I find it refreshing how your passion and purpose can ignite an urgency inside you that warms the heart when extended.

Let me enlighten the reader by saying that not all homeless persons are drug addicts, rapists, or violent people. Homelessness is a crude and disturbing state for any human being. However, judgment is eliminated only when you seek to know more about a person and what led to his or her current situation. I am reminded of two homeless persons with whom I developed a friendship, and I made a commitment to feed and talk with them daily while working in the metropolitan area. Each of these homeless men, though from opposite spectrums of life, had a story of how his or her life was disrupted and ended up on the vicious streets of destitution.

In most cases, a passerby would never understand a homeless person's unfortunate situation just by looking at him or her. There is a popular saying that "most people are one paycheck away from homelessness." That statement is true for many, but if we cannot relate to the situation in the present, we tend to exempt ourselves from that state of being. Life has served some bitter medicine to people who have found themselves in unfortunate conditions that caused embarrassment, sickness, and grief. We should all be grateful for a reasonable life and also be kind to our fellow men, who have experienced the woes of life. Be humble. Be kind. Be wise. Be appreciated. Eliminate pride. Avoid the urge to be arrogant with your treasures, talents, and fame, because life has a subtle but potent way of teaching humility and grace.

The first homeless man was a descendant of Africa, who migrated to North America and worked for years at a factory. Unfortunately, during the recession, the economy failed, and his place of employment was permanently closed. At that time, jobs of a similar nature were difficult to attain, and that eventually caused him to lose his home and belongings, thereby robbing him of his dignity. His close friends tried to help in whatever way they could, but after a while, he had to fend for himself. The harsh reality is that well-meaning acquaintances will help you to a point, but no one is willing to carry another person's burden for a long period of time, no matter the cause. He never had a chance to contact his family overseas and eventually took to the streets for refuge. He told me he refused the nearby shelters because he feared sexual abuse and drug overdose, so this desolate man walked to the metropolitan area every day, sat quietly while reading his inspirational books, and prayed for a breakthrough. He became a permanent subject in the area; folks fed him, chatted with him, and empathized with his situation, but eventually he died on the streets and was buried by the state. This is a sad story of life's mishaps, but it teaches us to help each other along the way, because we just never know when the table can turn.

The second homeless man was Caucasian, who walked the streets for years barefoot, malnourished, and mute. He had a snobbish and prideful countenance, and he never accepted food from anyone. Many times folks got offended and judged him without knowing his reasons for rejecting a kind gesture,

59

but interestingly, no one ventured to engage him either. I was concerned about his condition. I silently prayed for him, and after contemplating the matter for weeks, I approached him because something deep within felt the need to reach out to him. I later found out this gentleman was a professional from a wealthy family; he had a protracted legal battle over a family inheritance and lost everything. He was hurt, damaged, and angry from his past stories; and he shared with me that he would never discuss the depth of his story with anyone. He said he was homeless by choice, and none of his family members knew where he was. He alluded to the fact that many wondered about his choice of meals but that he was diabetic and ate certain fruits only to sustain his health. Unfortunately, this gentleman later died of a diabetic coma and was also buried by the state. I share these stories to show the world that life is impartial, and none of us, regardless of our upbringing or socioeconomic status, are exempt from unforeseen circumstances of life.

Over the years, my passion to help the powerless gave birth to my annual Give Back events. One of my favorite was honoring senior citizens in the community. Life is a challenge for all age-groups amid the turmoil around us; it takes discipline, courage, and determination to survive to the senior years. Our planet is deteriorating; hence there is mankind's struggle with obstacles that attack our immune system, physical being, and mental state. We are masked with unexplainable health problems caused from the foods we eat to environmental problems such as poor air quality, the rising sea level, and global warming. It should be noted that our senior citizens are favored with wisdom, experience, and strength; it was a joy to honor them with gifts, proclamations, and adoration.

Children are our future, and I find it rewarding to invest in these innocent and promising souls, to make a positive impact on society. Another favorite event was my Disney shindig for an elementary school, where I created an environment of fun, excitement, and laughter, with themes of the popular Minnie and Mickey Mouse characters. It was a pleasure to witness how the children were overjoyed and happy to play, dance along, and enjoy the Disney memorabilia. Showing love and creating harmony to the lives of children create indelible memories they will cherish for years to come. When we invest in children, we never really know for certain what positive impact we are creating, but the calculated aggregate is that overall, we are making a positive contribution to the future leaders of tomorrow.

I love to participate in mission trips and travel to impoverished countries to lend a helping hand to those who are underprivileged and unable to physically, emotionally, or financially support themselves or their families. I can recall my first mission to South America, which changed my life forever. The poverty, neglect, and distress all around were disheartening, but the image that captured my heart was the amazement of how little these people possessed, yet they carried a countenance of gratitude and happiness just to be alive. This experience forced me to reevaluate my priorities and focus on what is most important—the gift of life. Since that indelible excursion, I have become more appreciative and less concerned with the futile pleasures of life. These gestures of caring and sharing for others serve as outlets to nurture my passion and purpose to care. It is during these occasions that I am afforded the opportunity to minister love and attention to the sick, lame, hungry, lonely, and disabled. Extending my love and support to others is the pinnacle to my ultimate goal to touch as many lives and create a legacy. This makes my life worth living.

Know that your purpose will find you. Listen to your heart and identify the thing that draws you in. My beautiful niece found her passion in liturgical praise dancing. She acquired the skill from her mother, a professional praise dancer; however, it was her passion that allowed her to embrace the strong emotion of spiritual formations. Her routine is purpose driven, and it captivates the audience in a soul-searching type of atmosphere. In an effortless demeanor, she flows with the spirit and allows the depth of her performance to enthrall the air in an almost-divine encounter with the creator. Seek to connect with the passion that engulfs your purpose in life. Don't just live your life aimlessly; remember, we are never fulfilled until we are walking in our purpose.

Chapter 8

Faith in Truth

Through hard work, perseverance and faith
in God, you can live your dreams.

—Ben Carson

*H*aving a personal relationship with God through prayer, meditating, and giving to others are fulfilling qualities to which everyone can give full participation. The truth is, we are all aware that there is a higher being who controls the universe. In whatever form we envision this God, let us be quiet and reflect on the divine power, because only God holds the destiny of our lives. Find the synergy that brings peace and tranquility to your soul. Learn to be content in every state you find yourself, and purpose in your heart that living your dreams is a deliberate act.

A few years ago, I had a longing for more, I craved something deeper in the spiritual realm, so I sought God for direction and later found a place where my spirit man could connect and thrive. If you wholeheartedly search, you will ultimately find that divine connection that satisfies your soul and mind. Nothing is wrong with changing association and satisfying the hunger of your soul. As a matter of fact, it is a healthy practice philosophers and clerics encourage worldwide. If we get complacent and settle for mediocrity, we are essentially robbing our lives of what God intended for us. Connecting with your faith is enough to heal you from physical, mental, and emotional ailments. In my lifetime, I have heard, read, and witnessed folks being healed miraculously and later testifying that their deliverance was solely achieved from believing and leaning on their faith in God.

Take, for instance, my father, a loving, kindhearted, unassuming gentleman with an admirable persona and a heart of gold. At eighty-plus years, my father has endured many physical challenges to both his body and mind, but his faith in God undoubtedly delivered him on numerous occasions. Years ago my father battled and survived cancer, bowel obstruction, and many transient ischemic attacks, better known as "minor strokes." But Dad was fervent that none of those physical attacks would curtail his mission in life. As an entrepreneur and spiritual visionary, Dad was determined to fulfill his purpose on earth. But later in life, glaucoma, the disease that caused increased pressure in his eyes that later robbed him of his sight, attacked him. This was a trauma that affected the entire family, because in addition to being a businessman, my father was also a striving agriculturist who grew and provided organic produce to his family and the community. Blindness can denote a negative connotation simply because it robs a person of vision; but on a positive note, blindness doesn't rob a person of the gift of life. Although this impairment crippled my dad's ability to enjoy the beauty of nature, to indulge in his hobbies, to watch his grandchildren grow, and to see the face of his beautiful wife, Dad persevered and pushed beyond his obvious disability. My father quickly accepted his situation and willed in his heart to maximize his other senses to make the best of his life. A true inspiration and fighter, even though he couldn't see, my dad was able to accomplish many challenges. Dad learned how to operate his talking watch, mastered the features of his television and CD player, and continued to enjoy his routine morning walks to maintain his physical strength and also to minister to folks he would meet along the way.

As you have read or heard, my father, now in his late eighties, has acquired many testimonies of hope and faith, which have ultimately strengthened our faith to hold fast without wavering. But his challenges weren't yet over. Most recently, the incident that perplexed and saddened the family and his entire colleagues was when my father was stricken with yet another life-threatening disease that placed him in a coma. This seemed like the final test. The nurses gave up, and the doctor advised all the children and relatives to come home for his vigil. We cried, we prayed, and we all urgently converged at his bedside … but God had a plan to show Himself mighty.

Music is life, and Dad has a passion for songs that revive the spirit and quicken the soul. While my father lay still in his comatose state, we played songs of praise continuously, especially Dad's favorite song, "It is a Beautiful Day" by songwriter Jermaine Edwards. Even though all his vitals indicated that the end was near and the nurses kept wondering when his demise would come, we stretched our faith on Dad's behalf and continued playing the same song over and over again. Miraculously, in the wee hours of this particular night at the hospital while the song was playing, we noticed Dad was tapping his fingers and trying to sing the words. We were amazed, and then suddenly Dad got up from his deep slumber and clearly demanded that he wanted to pray. See, my father is of Cuban ancestry, and during that moment his Latin accent was distinct as he uttered a few words in Spanish and started to sing aloud with his hands in the air, giving praise to God. Oh, what a jubilee it was in that hospital room. We had mixed emotions. It was frightening. It was overwhelming, and for all of us, it was joyful. Immediately, those of us who were staying with him at the hospital called and woke up the other family members so they too could talk with him and witness the miraculous awakening.

Today, I can report that my dad is alive and well; and he is grateful to be a recipient of God's love, mercy, and grace. It was not many days after my dad was discharged from the hospital that he was out in the community, praying for the sick and encouraging others. The journey of my dad's life is nothing short of a miracle to remind the world that life is certainly a gift and that no matter what the circumstances may be, your willpower and faith are powerful vessels to revive any dormant situation in your life. My family found our truth in Jesus Christ. Even though this painful ordeal nagged our spirits, in the end it was our faith in Him that gave us the victory. It was nothing special about my father, but grace and truth were sufficient to deliver him from the window of death.

Your truth is important. Your faith will have a profound effect on your survival in life, so take some time to identify your faith. All along the journey, deep within his heart, my father had the will to live. We must inhabit that insatiable appetite that forces our spirit to want to preserve life, even when the ring of darkness and death seems imminent. Know this—none of us will leave this earth until our appointed time, so let us commit to someone bigger than our ego and aim to fulfill our dreams and aspirations, because countless life experiences have revealed that there is obviously truth in faith. Find your truth in someone or something that can move mountains and has a proven track record to perform supernaturally. Only then will your life find divine happiness, joy, and peace.

Chapter 9

Color Your Life—It's Worth It

Believe that life is worth living and your belief
will help create the fact.

—William James

*C*oloring your life is simply making every moment count. It's the conscious quest to make your life more beautiful, enjoyable, and worthwhile. Let me reiterate that you should live your life with the seal "No regrets." Your life is essentially your world. Your life is your domain. Traveling the world is the path that teaches us how to appreciate our own lives and reminds us not to judge what we don't understand. Exploring nature geographically throughout the world embodies the beauty of nature. Delving into another culture, activity, religion, or even a routine is superior to understanding the parameters that define the crux or magnitude of the challenges involved.

Understand that there is an array of activities that can be used to color our lives. Paint, markers, or crayons are all coloring tools known to make whatever they attach themselves to more appealing, beautiful, and permanent. Let us identify the coloring tools that can enhance our individual worlds and improve our lives. Reject the tendency to limit your mind. Move beyond the norm of your understanding or tradition. Pursue what speaks to your senses and emotions. Be eclectic. Wear bold colors. Explore dressing beyond the cultural barriers. Why not? Life is what you make it. There are really no defined rules to coloring your world.

Color your world at any age by sharpening your mental agility. Learn to relax. Smile at silly jokes, create snow angels or sandcastles, and just lighten up. Your brain deserves it. Change your mind-set and enhance your intellect. God never intended us to be narrow minded, so appreciate the differences around you. Try different cuisines and revive your palate. Listen to a new genre and caress your soul. Learn another language and challenge your brain. Go people watching and enjoy the complexity of choices. Lend a helping hand and make someone smile. Always remember that courage and willpower are important attributes that can plateau our lives into something amazing, interesting, and admired.

Color your world by taking better care of yourself. No matter your age, you can be more selective with healthier lifestyle choices that eventually will make you healthier and happier, of course affording you a more productive life. Adults, listen to your bodies. Refrain from the temptation to overindulge. Follow up with your annual checkups. Amid your busy schedules, if it's time to take a break, go ahead and seize the moment. Go the extra mile to make healthier meal choices. You don't necessarily have to become the staunch vegan. Incorporate light exercises. Take ample rest. These are just a few simple, timeless tricks that can improve the quality of your life. Personally, I am coloring my world by drinking more water. I'm not a fan of the bland taste; however, I understand the long-term health benefits of consuming enough of the crystal medicine. Feeling good from within ultimately reflects on the outside. Your personality radiates. You appreciate and smile at the little things.

A gratifying practice that is common in this twenty-first century is giving back. Feel free to extend to others and not only tangible items. Practice patience, tolerance, and forgiveness. Donating our time, energy, money, or even our belongings is a fulfilling gesture that can be used to color our lives. Extending happiness to another person, an organization, or a country far exceeds being selfish or restricting our kindness to a particular area. If we stop to think, we see that each of us is a beneficiary of kindness. We know how refreshing it feels to receive a gift, a hug, or even valuable advice. It's never too late to shine and explore the inner diamonds inside our heart chambers. Let us search our souls to unearth the hidden treasures that can help to brighten an imperfect world.

Color your life by adopting and nurturing a person or pet. I have five four-legged friends and have found that their love and loyalty are satisfying and irrefutable. Loving without boundaries is life changing. Social science research has proved that there are psychological correlations to health and mental benefits of having pets. Pets offer a special type of companionship and can detect the emotions of their owners, whether a child, an elderly person, or just a lonely person. Invest in the pet of your choice. After all, they are placed in the universe to add beauty and joy to our lives.

One of my favorite rituals to color my world is observing birthdays, which are indicative of added life and another year to evaluate and change for the better. Birthdays should be celebrated, especially milestones. I am not only referring to the obvious sixteen, eighteen, twenty-one, fifty, sixty-five, or one hundred. Milestones should mean any number that is significant to you. That number could be the age when your loved one recovered from a disease or addiction or the age when you always desired to attain a specific goal. Whatever your reason to make it super special, make it happen. Suggestions are always welcoming, but the deciding factors remain with you. Take a trip if you can. Make your favorite meal. Gather with old friends. Visit an institution to give back. Lounge around in your favorite pajamas. Whatever is special to you, just do it. Remember, you are in control of your life. Celebrate your way. So whether you are a parent, spouse, child, or sibling, feel free to surprise your loved ones on their birthdays; this notion that some folks express about not wanting the fuss on their birthday is simply a fallacy. For the record, everyone who breathes desires the joy to feel loved and appreciated. Some might be accustomed to this treat, but I believe in the long run, recognition and adoration are always welcome. Take pictures to capture the moments, because one day these will become heirlooms, which future generations will certainly appreciate.

Whatever you can perceive, make it happen. You are the only hindrance to coloring your world. As one of my twin sisters usually says, "Call it," a positive precept that denotes that in whatever you wish to achieve, just go for it. Speak it into existence. Yes, your words have power, but you have to activate those words with enthusiasm and action. Let your inner being search for the fire within your soul and allow it to soar and take you to greater heights. Be grateful for everything, and remember that the thing you take for granted—whether life, peace, family, or food— someone else is wishing he or she had it.

Find your inner strength. Pursue peace and face reality. In order to maximize your full potential, you must forgive and forget. Learn to foster positivity, love, and gratitude. Remember the popular cliché that your life may not come with a red bow, but it is still special and deserves to be cherished and appreciated. Capture moments, take pictures, and make videos because it is really these "little" things that color our world. Share the contents of this short but purposeful handbook with anyone you meet so we can all level up to whom and what God intended us to be.

Final word: Make a commitment to remove yourself from the facade of what everyone thinks you should be. Aspire to be you. Find your happy place. Dare to be happy and live your best life ever.

About the Author

Sheridon, affectionately called Donna, is a multitalented, inspiring, passionate, and spiritual young lady from the beautiful Caribbean island of Jamaica. She carries the spirit of her deceased Hispanic grandmother, Alicia Francia, whom she prides as her guiding angel. Donna spent most of her childhood summer days with her grandparents and gleaned valuable attributes and habits from their humble lifestyle.

A born leader at the early age of twelve, Donna started her first girls' club, which she casually called "Pearl." Her siblings and neighbors gathered weekly to practice arts and crafts, knitting, crocheting, and cooking. Items the girls made were sold at her dad's store for small rewards. Pearls are said to lift the spirits and give a feeling of calm, beauty, and dignity. How coincidental that as an adult, Donna regularly adorns herself in beautiful pearls as a symbol of her sophisticated life. She enjoys putting smiles on faces and strongly believes that expressing love and gratitude has been the most rewarding quality of her life.

Donna is a professional in the corporate world, a certified motivational speaker, and holds a master's degree from a reputable university in North America. Her daily prayer is to see people live the best of their lives.

In the end, it's not the years in your *life* that
count, but it's the *life* in your years.
—Abraham Lincoln

Author's Note

Be happy for this moment. This moment is your life.

—Omar Khayyam

Amid the chaos, conflicts, disappointments, and fear, this purposeful book, simply titled *Life … You Can Do It: Coloring Your World through Adversity*, is designed to enrich, empower and enlighten you on the intricacies of life. Life is paramount, and the decisions we make with our lives determine our happiness and ultimately shape our destiny. At fifty-plus years old, I have had my fair share of mishaps, hiccups, and bruises, but I am grateful to be in the land of the living, still walking on planet earth. Disappointments taught me determination. Pain taught me hope. Mistakes taught me wisdom. Mishaps taught me perseverance. I have learned to be content in every situation, not to have anxiety, and in all things to express love, show gratitude, and cherish life daily. This is the ideal book to help you appreciate your life, focus on the positive elements, and strive for what you deserve in life.

This book is also available in audio for easy listening to soothe the brain of the comatose patient, encourage the person on the verge of suicide, comfort the parent making life-altering decisions, help the addict struggling to recover, enlighten the visually impaired of the beauty of life, encourage the person who has lost in love, or accompany the busy executive commuting for hours. Reading this book will make you laugh, cry, praise, learn, reflect, deflect, and appreciate the blessing of being alive. I dare you to follow me on this beautiful journey called "life."